IMAGES
of America

AFRICAN AMERICANS
IN SPRINGFIELD

The John Hay Homes were named after one of Pres. Abraham Lincoln's Civil War secretaries. In 1941, the two-story brick units could house up to 2,500 tenants and contained sidewalks, parking lots, playgrounds, landscaping, a community room, and an administration building. They spanned Eleventh to Sixteenth Streets and Madison to Reynolds Streets. The US Housing Authority provided funding. (Courtesy of Sangamon Valley Collection at Lincoln Library.)

ON THE COVER: Taken in the 1940s by professional photographer Doc Helm, this image shows the Palm Room on the fourth floor of the Hotel Abraham Lincoln. Located on Fifth Street and Capitol Avenue, the hotel operated from 1925 to 1964 and hired African Americans. Many lawmakers and celebrities were guests, and Marguerite Taborn (far right), along with three unidentified colleagues, would have served them. (Beverly Helm-Renfro.)

IMAGES
of America

AFRICAN AMERICANS
IN SPRINGFIELD

Mary Frances and Beverly Helm-Renfro

ARCADIA
PUBLISHING

Published by Arcadia Publishing
Charleston, South Carolina

Printed in the United States of America

Library of Congress Control Number: 2022933234

For all general information, please contact Arcadia Publishing:
Telephone 843-853-2070
Fax 843-853-0044
E-mail sales@arcadiapublishing.com
For customer service and orders:
Toll-Free 1-888-313-2665

Visit us on the Internet at www.arcadiapublishing.com

*To the black families, celebrities, ordinary people, organizations,
service groups, friends, churches, and businesses in Springfield
that thrived from the 1800s to 1970s and beyond.*

CONTENTS

ACKNOWLEDGMENTS

Mary Frances wants to thank her coauthor Beverly Helm-Renfro, editor Caitrin Cunningham, local historian Curtis Mann who reviewed this book, and everyone who provided photographs and information to make this book happen.

Beverly Helm-Renfro wants to acknowledge her father, Eddie Winfred "Doc" Helm, for preserving the history of black life in Springfield. All images credited to her were originally from his personal collection. She thanks all the other contributors to this labor of love and to Mary Frances for working with her as the coauthor to bring this important history to life. Thank you, Arcadia Publishing.

INTRODUCTION

This book contains seven chapters about African Americans in Springfield, Illinois. The chapters cover art and education, civic engagement, employment, entrepreneurship, military and public safety, politics, and the Springfield Urban League. Within the chapters is a progression from Reconstruction to Jim Crow to civil rights, showing how lives changed. Segregation and desegregation, important components of this history, left indelible legacies.

The photographs range from 1886 to 1975. Locally known professional photographers such as Guy Mathis, Herbert Georg, and Doc Helm took most of them. Only relevant, original photographs were scanned and used. Sources were dispersed throughout Springfield in archives, individual collections, libraries, and museums. Information for captions came from academic records, books, cemetery records, census data, city directories, maps, newspapers, obituaries, and personal recollections.

The earliest photograph is a vignette bust portrait of an unidentified man created in 1886 by Dennis Williams. Williams migrated from Mississippi to Springfield during the Civil War. He exhibited at the Illinois State Fair and established a prolific career as an artist with studios on the downtown square. However, like many of the African Americans in this book, he could have been placed in multiple chapters. He was an entrepreneur, community activist, and Republican party supporter. If he had lived longer, he may have taught art classes at the Springfield Urban League. The latest photographs show professors, staff, and students at Sangamon State University, created in 1970.

In the art and education chapter are painters, dancers, and musicians who were self-taught, took correspondence courses, or attended universities. One painter graduated from Lincoln University in Missouri, which was created by African American Civil War soldiers to benefit other freed blacks. Some of them exhibited at the state fair and instructed art classes at Douglass Community Center. Others established their own businesses or worked for government agencies. Some traveled, fostering their careers in other cities and states.

Springfield public schools became integrated in 1873, yet independent schools catering to African Americans continued into the 1940s. Some of them were created and staffed by African Americans using Booker T. Washington's Tuskegee Institute model. The Springfield Urban League offered classes for its nursery school students. Sangamon State University, from its inception, continued this legacy by hiring African American faculty. Faculty, staff, and students went on to establish a caucus and student support services.

The civic engagement chapter revolves around national, state, and local organizations. The National Association for the Advancement of Colored People (NAACP), Illinois Association of Colored Women's Clubs, Illinois Workers Alliance, Frontiers International, Boy Scouts, House of Kings, and East End Neighborhood Club are examples. Many of their leaders were highly regarded professionals represented in other chapters. For example, Charles Lockhart coached Golden Gloves boxers and was also a Springfield fireman for 37 years.

The chapter on employment covers a wide range of professions, including archivist, artist, bricklayer, butler, concrete pourer, cook, electrical worker, elevator operator, factory worker, insurance agent, journalist, laborer, laundry worker, librarian, maid, package wrapper, pastor, porter, public school teacher, salesman, shoemaker, waitress, and whitewasher. Some of them attended universities in Illinois; others attended historically black colleges and universities around the country. Early photographs show evidence of child labor, and later images depict workers breaking the color barrier. Some employees worked at hotels where African Americans were not permitted to stay. Others went on to become entrepreneurs.

Entrepreneurs ran businesses primarily on the east side of Springfield where the African American population was concentrated. Businesses in this chapter include a barbershop, beauty salon, brothel, café, car showroom, cocktail lounge, dentist, dry cleaner, gas station, family physician, farm, funeral home, greenhouse, hotel, real estate agency, shoe shine parlor, tavern, and trucking business. Some of the businesses survived the Great Depression and became popular meeting places for African Americans. Still others catered to state fair visitors and travelers using *The Negro Motorist Green Book*. One entrepreneur traveled around the country marketing his automobile invention—a compressed air motor that ran without gasoline.

Some of the earlier photographs in this book are in the military and public safety chapter. In 1898, the 8th Illinois Infantry served in San Luis, Cuba, during the Spanish-American War. Because both soldiers and officers were African American, they had to endure skepticism from the United States and Cuba. Earlier soldiers, such as Charles Grandy and James Lewis, celebrated their Civil War service by attending annual Grand Army of the Republic encampments in Springfield.

Some soldiers later became firemen, city police officers, and state police officers. Firemen were stationed primarily at the segregated Firehouse No. 5 on the east side. City police officers had contentious careers and endured repeated scrutiny and corrective action. However, they persevered and some were promoted. Illinois state police officers came from all over Illinois and trained in Springfield. They worked with new radar technology, competed in pistol matches at the state fairgrounds, and recruited minority youth as part of affirmative action.

Because Springfield is the state capital and home of Abraham Lincoln, many African American leaders came here to work as politicians and commemorate the accomplishments of our 16th president. The Illinois State Capitol, Illinois Governor's Mansion, Democratic State Central Committee of Illinois headquarters, and Lincoln's tomb became meaningful places to gather for a photograph. Governors in these photographs include Dwight Green, Richard Yates Jr., Adlai Stevenson, William Stratton, and Otto Kerner. Illinois struggled with implementation of federal and state laws regarding minority employment, and in 1958, Floy Clements became the first African American woman elected to the Illinois General Assembly.

Finally, the Springfield Urban League was housed in a magnificent historic building that served African Americans for many years and in many ways. The league held picnics for the elderly, conferences for youth, and annual banquets featuring national speakers. It awarded scholarships for high schoolers ready to attend college, strove for more African Americans in the workplace, and recognized local businesses exhibiting positive racial hiring practices. The league encouraged sports, music, good health, and racial tolerance.

Lifelong Springfield residents, migrants from the South, visitors from Africa, and famous African Americans from around the country are in this book. They endured segregation and racism yet still obtained higher education, built careers, raised families, and gave back to their community. Many of the buildings they worked and gathered in are now gone. However, their creativity, compassion, intelligence, strength, and resilience remain and are memorialized in this book.

One

ART AND EDUCATION

Hiram Jackson graduated from Lincoln University in Missouri in 1938. He also taught art there. As an oil, water, and pastel painter, he won prizes at the Illinois State Fair and led classes at Douglass Community Center. In 1935, the Springfield NAACP awarded him a plaque of honor. He was later hired as staff artist at the *Illinois State Journal* newspaper. (Beverly Helm-Renfro.)

Dennis Williams was a prolific and well-respected African American artist during the 1870s and 1880s in Springfield. He worked from studios downtown on the state capitol square and created portraits of politicians, families, businessmen, and the deceased. In this 1886 portrait of an unidentified man, Williams's faint signature can be seen above the left shoulder. Only four Williams portraits are known to exist; two are in Springfield. (Courtesy of Illinois State Museum.)

Louis Evans directed the Springfield Colored Municipal Band in the 1940s. The band played at parades, churches, Lake Springfield Fourth of July celebrations, and here at the Douglass Community Center at Fifteenth and Monroe Streets. The band had approximately 24 members. Evans was also a member of the executive board of the Musicians Protective Union No. 675. (Courtesy of Springfield Urban League Inc.)

Eddie Winfred "Doc" Helm was born in 1911 in Mount Vernon, Illinois, and moved to Springfield in 1934. Ten years later, he became Illinois's official state photographer as an employee of the secretary of state. He also worked from a darkroom in his basement at 1128 South Pasfield Street as well as a commercial studio at 809 East Washington Street. (Beverly Helm-Renfro.)

Charles Maxwell (far left) was born in Springfield in 1878 and worked as a custodian, landscape gardener, musician, and parade leader for over 40 years. He became a member of the 8th Illinois Infantry, Company I, and won five medals for his military service, which included the Spanish-American War. Known as the "Springfield Bugler," he is pictured here in 1943 at Abraham Lincoln's tomb. (Courtesy of Abraham Lincoln Presidential Library and Museum.)

In 1941, Ruth Fortune began offering free tap dance classes through the Douglass Community Center at 234 South Fifteenth Street. Children between 10 and 18 years old were invited and performed as the Ruth Fortune Dancers. Fortune had studied for three years with Ruth Davis of Taylorville. The Douglass Community Center was dismantled in the 1950s as part of desegregation efforts in Springfield. (Beverly Helm-Renfro.)

This is a Singleton wedding during the 1950s. Doc Helm took correspondence courses in photography and filled the niche of African American commercial photographer in Springfield for over 50 years. Weddings, along with many other aspects of African American life, were part of his freelance work. (Beverly Helm-Renfro.)

John "Happy" Green (first row, far right) was born in Carmi, Illinois, and moved to Springfield in 1921. He married Betty Jean Picket-Thomas (first row, center), and they formed the duo Happy Green and Betty Jean, playing at Stevie's Latin Village, Mansion View Motel, and St. Nicholas Hotel. Green also played with the 4-Clefs, who toured the country from the 1930s to the 1950s. (Beverly Helm-Renfro.)

Marvin Jackson grew up in the John Hay Homes in the 1950s, and after musical stints in San Francisco and Nashville, he returned to Springfield and formed the Ebonies. From left to right are Arlene Williams, Jackson, and Roy Williams, who performed soul, rhythm and blues, and love ballads throughout the Midwest. In interviews, Jackson commented on the segregation he experienced in the music industry. (Beverly Helm-Renfro.)

George Pierson (left) and Etta Moten perform for 400 people at a benefit concert for the Springfield Urban League held in the Springfield High School auditorium on June 27, 1950. Moten was an internationally known stage, screen, and concert performer. The pair performed African American spirituals, German songs, and classical works by Bach, Schubert, List, Debussy, and Tchaikovsky. They gave a 30-minute encore. (Courtesy of Springfield Urban League Inc.)

The Ambidexter Industrial School was created by African American Springfield residents and operated from 1901 to 1908 at 902 South Twelfth Street. Local and out-of-town male and female students attended. Academics, art, and trades were taught using Booker T. Washington's Tuskegee

Institute as a model. It relied solely on donations from churches, businesses, and individuals. (Courtesy of Sangamon Valley Collection at Lincoln Library.)

Beginning in 1859, African Americans in Springfield had their own school. After 1873, they could attend any public school. Here are six unidentified African American students (second and third rows) in the Iles School's graduating class of 1931. Iles School was dedicated in 1893 on East Laurel Street and had well water, coal heat, and a library accessible to everyone in the school district. (Courtesy of Abraham Lincoln Presidential Library and Museum.)

Here is an unidentified group of women and children at the Springfield Urban League nursery school. In 1934, there were 20 students in nursery school classes with Imogene Mosely and Hazel Scott as instructors. Jeremiah Hill offered adult classes in Spanish, English, American history, African American history, math, and economics. The organization was also planning classes for domestic and personal service workers. (Courtesy of Springfield Urban League Inc.)

The Carver Trade School opened in 1946 and offered training in linotyping, typesetting, and typecasting for African American GIs. It was created in a partnership between the Springfield Urban League at 234 South Fifteenth Street and Foster Printing Company at 1210 South Sixteenth

Street. The first 20-month class had 12 students who met from 9:00 a.m. to 3:00 p.m. (Courtesy of Springfield Urban League Inc.)

Mark Conley (center) received a bachelor's degree from Arkansas Agricultural, Mechanical, and Normal College and a master's degree from New Mexico State University, and became a charter faculty member at Sangamon State University in 1970. Conley taught a course called Mood of Black America, which was the first course at the university addressing African American issues. (Courtesy of Brookens Library.)

Pictured are, from left to right, Augustine Stevens, Tia Stevens, and Adalina Stevens in the 1970s. Augustine Stevens was a native of Sierra Leone and assistant professor of political studies at Sangamon State University in 1974. He had a bachelor's degree in philosophy, a master's degree in international relations from Northwestern University, and an expected doctorate degree in comparative politics. (Courtesy of Brookens Library.)

Homer Butler was born in 1932 in Trenton, New Jersey, and attended Temple University and Sangamon State University. He served as vice chancellor for student affairs at Sangamon State University from 1970 to 1996. Many community groups, including the NAACP, benefited from his membership and leadership. (Courtesy of Brookens Library.)

In March 1973, Sangamon State University's Black Student Union held Black Awareness Week. Called A Journey into Black Culture, the event highlighted political, economic, and social issues relating to African Americans. Here, civil rights activist, peace activist, and comedian Dick Gregory addresses students and the public in the cafeteria of the main campus. (Courtesy of Brookens Library.)

In 1975, the Minority Service Center at Sangamon State University held a social gathering at 1320 East Reynolds Street, which was home to the Springfield Housing Authority and John Hay Homes recreation center. All university minority students were invited to attend the five-hour gathering. Seen here are three members of the organization. (Courtesy of Brookens Library.)

Two

CIVIC ENGAGEMENT

In 1963, demonstrators gathered in front of the Abraham Lincoln statue at the Illinois State Capitol. They held signs concerning civil rights, surplus food programs, rent allowance, prejudice in employment, freedom to work, and a living wage. On August 28 of that year, Rev. Martin Luther King Jr. addressed approximately 200,000 civil rights demonstrators at the United States Capitol. (Courtesy of Illinois State Archives, Doc Helm Collection.)

Two men extinguish smoldering ashes after the Springfield Race Riot of 1908. Local reporters asked anti-lynching crusader Ida Wells if she would hold an indignation meeting, but she believed no one would host it. This motivated her to create the Negro Fellowship League to study the criminalization of African Americans. In 1910, the league opened a reading room and social center at 2830 State Street in Chicago. (Courtesy of Abraham Lincoln Presidential Library and Museum.)

In 1936, the Illinois Workers Alliance held a hunger march in Douglas Park. After meeting with Gov. Henry Horner, they encamped at the park where local police ordered them to stay within park limits or leave the city. They were part of the Workers Alliance of America, founded by the Socialist Party of America in 1935 to bring relief to workers employed by the Works Progress Administration. (Courtesy of Abraham Lincoln Presidential Library and Museum.)

In 1941, Gov. Dwight Green (right) meets with W.E.B. Du Bois in the governor's office. Du Bois had just published *Dusk of Dawn*, his second autobiography. Shortly after this visit, Du Bois was dismissed from Atlanta University and subsequently worked for the NAACP, which was formed in response to publicity from the Springfield Race Riot of 1908. (Beverly Helm-Renfro.)

On Abraham Lincoln's 136th birthday in 1945, the NAACP held a dinner with Illinois representative Charles Jenkins as speaker. The next day, the Illinois General Assembly met in a joint session to hear Roscoe Simmons speak. He was a Chicago Republican orator and the first African American to address a combined legislative group in Illinois. The speakers, along with Herbert Wells Fay (fourth from left), custodian of Lincoln's tomb, pose at the tomb. (Courtesy of Abraham Lincoln Presidential Library and Museum.)

Harry Eielson was a gifted athlete at Springfield High School, at Northwestern University, and in the US Navy. He returned to Springfield and became county treasurer, county sheriff, Springfield commissioner for health and safety, and mayor from 1947 to 1951. This picture was taken in the 1940s, most likely when Eielson was mayor and encouraged sports teams such as the Wiz Kids. (Beverly Helm-Renfro.)

In the 1950s, a Frontiers International member awards Sandra Kirk a camera as first prize in a talent show, which likely occurred at the Douglass Community Center. In 1951, Kirk also participated in a craft program at the center, which involved transforming scraps and discarded objects into functional decorations. In 1961, she graduated from Feitshans High School. (Courtesy of Springfield Urban League Inc.)

The East End Neighborhood Club was officially established in 1927 and remained active throughout the 1950s. Here, the club meets for a tea at the Springfield Urban League building at 234 South Fifteenth Street. Events included fish fries, moonlight picnics, entertainment at the Lincoln Colored Home, zinnia flower bed contests, lamp making, domestic fairs, and talks on social hygiene. (Courtesy Springfield Urban League Inc.)

In 1952, an unidentified member (left) of the Illinois Association of Colored Women's Clubs donates a book to a staff member of the Illinois State Library at the Centennial building. Titles on the shelves behind them include *The Negro Caravan*, *The Master Slave*, *From Captivity to Fame*, and *Black Riot*. (Courtesy of Illinois State Archives, Doc Helm Collection.)

From left to right are Geraldine Lee, Roy Wilkins, Dr. Edwin Lee, and Phil Waring possibly attending the 35th Annual NAACP Lincoln-Douglass awards dinner held in 1956 at the Leland Hotel. Wilkins was executive secretary of the NAACP at this time and later served as executive director from 1964 to 1977. (Beverly Helm-Renfro.)

Taken in the mid-1950s, this image shows St. Paul African Methodist Episcopal Church Boy Scout Troop 37 with James Helm (far right), Doc Helm's son. The troop was organized at Stuart Street Christian Church located at Stuart and Sixteenth Streets and met on Thursday evenings. Scoutmasters and assistant scoutmasters led the meetings. (Beverly Helm-Renfro.)

Doc Helm liked to photograph his children James and Beverly with famous people who visited Springfield. World heavyweight boxing champion Joe Louis was one of those visitors. Louis was instrumental in integrating golf and poses here at a local course. In 1963, Springfield had two nine-hole golf courses, Bergen and Pasfield, and two 18-hole courses, Bunn Park and Lincoln Greens. (Beverly Helm-Renfro.)

From left to right are Julian Bond, Delores Marshall, and Proteon Penn socializing at a club in Springfield. Bond was a leader of the civil rights movement, politician, and first president of the Southern Poverty Law Center. He was also a leader of the NAACP. (Beverly Helm-Renfro.)

In 1960, Springfield's special citizens committee gathered food and clothing for 23,000 children cut off from government assistance in New Orleans, Louisiana. From left to right are Charles Spencer, Dr. Charles Young, Doris Robinson, Dr. Webster, and Dr. Edwin Lee. Robinson was an X-ray technician and member of the Mary Church Terrel Club, where she gave talks on health and hygiene. (Courtesy of Springfield Urban League Inc.)

In the 1960s, the Springfield Colored Women's Club held meetings in the community and recreation rooms of the John Hay Homes administrative building at 1320 East Reynolds Street. From left to right, Hattie Johnson, Bernice Reed, and three unidentified members auction off a package at an event. (Courtesy of Sangamon Valley Collection at Lincoln Library.)

The Springfield NAACP held its annual Lincoln-Douglass dinner at the Leland Hotel ballroom in 1965. From left to right are Raymond Harth, president of the Illinois chapter; Glenn Kniss, chairman of the banquet; and Dr. Aaron Henry, president of the Mississippi chapter. Over 400 people attended to hear Henry speak. (Courtesy of Sangamon Valley Collection at Lincoln Library.)

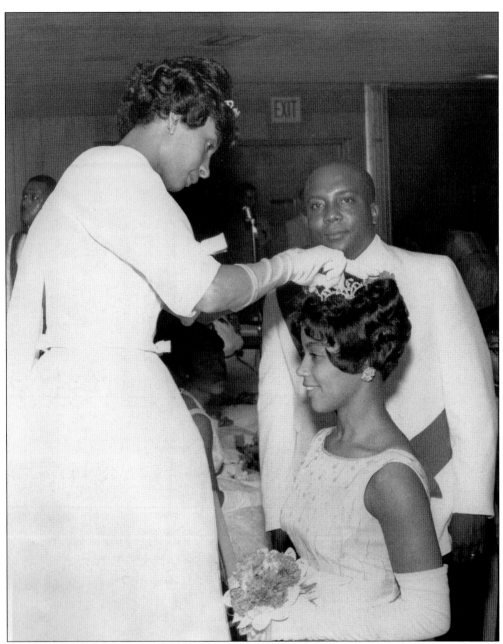

In 1965, the House of Kings was a civic organization serving African Americans through community engagement and scholarships. Its motto was "The Men Who Understand." Each year at a coronation ball, held either at the St. Nicholas Hotel or Allis-Chalmers banquet hall, the organization crowned a queen based on number of popularity votes sold. From left to right are outgoing queen Mary Ann Holmart, new queen Gloria Daugherty, and president Herbert Harris. (Courtesy of Sangamon Valley Collection at Lincoln Library.)

The year after winning the Nobel Peace Prize, Martin Luther King Jr. spoke in Springfield on October 7, 1965, at the eighth annual convention of the Illinois AFL-CIO held at the Illinois State Armory. King chastised the 4,000 delegates attending for not doing more to support the civil rights movement. He called for guaranteed annual wages, adequate minimum wages, and guaranteed employment for everyone willing to work. (Courtesy of Sangamon Valley Collection at Lincoln Library.)

At the Downtowner Motor Inn in 1967, Frontiers International officers were installed. From left to right are (first row) Dr. Charles Young, president; and Ivan Harper, vice president; (second row) James White, secretary; Harry Hale, treasurer; and Arthur Ferguson, executive board member. The organization held annual dinners as well as fish fries at Springfield Boy's Club at Fifteenth and Monroe Streets, donating proceeds to charity. (Courtesy of Sangamon Valley Collection at Lincoln Library.)

The Springfield NAACP held its annual Lincoln-Douglass dinner at Leland Hotel in 1967. From left to right are Alberta Brooks, Arthur Barnard, Charles Spencer, Mayor Nelson Howarth, and Julian Bond (Georgia House of Representatives). The Webster plaque, awarded for promoting better racial understanding and interracial progress, was presented to Mabel Meek. (Courtesy of Sangamon Valley Collection at Lincoln Library.)

Three

EMPLOYMENT

In 1965, car salesman Don Robinson (right) hands the keys over to an unidentified buyer of a Plymouth Belvidere at Railsplitters at Bypass 66 and Cook Street. In a 1965 advertisement in the *Daily Illinois State Register*, Robinson was pictured as the one African American salesman among seven white salesmen. (Courtesy of Springfield Urban League Inc.)

During the 1899 Illinois State Fair, carriages and bicycles decorated with sunflowers, chrysanthemums, roses, and poppies traveled through Springfield streets en route to the Springfield fairgrounds. Pictured here during the floral parade, two unidentified children lead Elizabeth Hampton and Inger Morgan to a dedication of the women's building during carnival week. Later, they attended an evening reception at the governor's mansion. (Courtesy of Abraham Lincoln Presidential Library and Museum.)

This unidentified child and Thomas Noblett of Noblett Laundry are pictured at 728 East Monroe Street. When this photograph was taken around 1900, the business was lucrative and Noblett may have employed African American children such as this one. (Courtesy of Abraham Lincoln Presidential Library and Museum.)

Around 1902, African American laborers are laying sewer in Washington Park west of MacArthur Boulevard and north of South Grand Avenue. Constructed in 1901, the park included an iron spring with water that was believed to have curative properties for ailments such as rheumatism, gout, and indigestion. Today, the park is listed in the National Register of Historic Places. (Courtesy of Abraham Lincoln Presidential Library and Museum.)

In 1902, an unidentified man whitewashes a fence in preparation for the Illinois State Fair. African Americans also set up exhibits for the fair and exhibited their own works. Dennis Williams, a prominent artist in the 1870s and 1880s, won first and second place for crayon portraits, pastel portraits, pencil drawings, India ink works, and animal paintings. (Courtesy of Abraham Lincoln Presidential Library and Museum.)

Many workers toiled long hours preparing for Illinois's 50th anniversary state fair held September 29 to October 4, 1902. The Chicago & Alton Railroad Company scheduled special excursion trains, resulting in record-breaking attendance. Exhibits included vegetables, livestock, machinery, and art. This unidentified worker rests on a barrel with a hammer in his hand at the Dome building. (Courtesy of Abraham Lincoln Presidential Library and Museum.)

In 1930, two men are working at Farris Furnace Company factory at Tenth Street and Enos Avenue. The company's automatic water-base furnace increased humidity, removed dust, and conserved heat. Examples of the furnace were exhibited at the Illinois State Fair and appeared in home rental and sale advertisements throughout Springfield. (Courtesy of Abraham Lincoln Presidential Library and Museum.)

In July 1932, an unidentified African American laborer (far left) lays brick on South Seventh Street for the Poston-Springfield Brick Company at 2600 South Grand Avenue East. Four months later, the company implemented a five-hour workday to spread employment among its 100 workers for a longer time, including the winter. This put less strain on the unemployment system during the Great Depression. (Courtesy of Abraham Lincoln Presidential Library and Museum.)

Dorothy Jeanette Mason Helm was born in 1916 in Springfield and worked at Allis-Chalmers Manufacturing Company as an assembly worker and at the Illini Country Club as a cook. She died in 1991 and is buried beside her husband, Doc Helm, in Oak Ridge Cemetery. They married in 1941. (Beverly Helm-Renfro.)

Around 1900, Henry Nelch & Son Co. opened at 921 East Jackson Street and later moved to 800 South Ninth Street. It sold premixed concrete and erected the first Ready Mix plant in Springfield. Here, one African American laborer helps pour concrete at a construction site in 1931. The company's concrete was used in state buildings, private businesses, homes, and sidewalks. (Courtesy of Abraham Lincoln Presidential Library and Museum.)

From left to right are Helen VanDiver, Gertrude Dant, and Shirley Stratton at the governor's mansion on September 2, 1953. Dant began working as a mansion cook in 1945. She lived at 1601 East Lawrence Avenue and was active in the Douglass Community Center and Union Baptist Church. Her éclair recipe was a favorite in local newspapers. (Courtesy of Sangamon Valley Collection at Lincoln Library.)

Joseph Tatum was born in 1897, became a private in the US Army during World War I, and later worked for Franklin Life Insurance Company. He died in 1975 and is buried in Camp Butler National Cemetery in Springfield. (Beverly Helm-Renfro.)

Earl Rice was born in 1930 in Mount Vernon, Illinois, and attended Langston University in Oklahoma. The university opened in 1897 with 41 students and today is the only historically black college or university in Oklahoma. After serving in the Army during the Korean War, Rice retired from Commonwealth Edison after a 30-year career. (Courtesy of Springfield Urban League Inc.)

Marie Porter Wheeler was born in 1913 in Metropolis, Illinois, and attended Southern Illinois State Normal University in Carbondale. By 1942, she had moved to Springfield and during World War II worked at the Sangamon Ordnance Plant in Illiopolis, where more than 60 percent of the employees were women. She retired from Allis-Chalmers Manufacturing Company in Springfield in 1969. (Courtesy of Brookens Library.)

The state senator from Chicago, Fred Smith (left), shakes hands with Simeon Osby, who grew up in Springfield and attended the University of Illinois Urbana-Champaign. He later returned to Springfield and created the *Capital City News*, an African American newspaper. He was a racial activist and active community member as well as correspondent for the *Chicago Defender*, an African American newspaper in Chicago. (Beverly Helm-Renfro.)

In 1897, while in his 20s, Bert Singleton began as a butler for Gov. John Tanner. Governors Richard Yates, Charles Deneen, Edward Dunne, Frank Lowden, Len Small, Louis Emmerson, Henry Horner, John Stelle, Dwight Green, and Adlai Stevenson followed. Singleton signed this photograph on December 20, 1947, during Green's administration. Singleton affectionately referred to governors as admirals and was loved for his warm smile and gracious service. (Courtesy of Sangamon Valley Collection at Lincoln Library.)

From left to right, Mattie Fowler, maid; Helen Van Diver, housekeeper; and Harry Burns, butler, stand in a governor's mansion room overlooking the Illinois State Capitol. Gov. William Stratton's leather desk stands in the foreground. Working at the mansion was a desirable job for minorities in Springfield during the Jim Crow era. (Courtesy of Sangamon Valley Collection at Lincoln Library.)

In 1955, Gilbert Wright serves Gov. William Stratton in the family dining room of the governor's mansion. Also pictured are Stratton's wife, Shirley, with her back to the camera, and daughters Diana (left) and Sandra. Wright was born in 1905 in Kentucky and was a butler at the mansion for 10 years before his untimely death shortly after this photograph was taken. (Courtesy of Abraham Lincoln Presidential Library and Museum.)

Robert Jones (left) began working as a butler at the governor's mansion in 1940. Here, he stands in the mansion kitchen in 1955 waiting to serve cake prepared by Gertrude Dant, mansion cook. Roberta Jones, daughter of Robert Jones, was a gifted contralto and performed spiritual songs such as "You'll Never Walk Alone" at the mansion. (Courtesy of Abraham Lincoln Presidential Library and Museum.)

Butlers William Hickman (left) and Wallace Jones arrange a 26-seat mahogany table in preparation for a tea in the state dining room of the governor's mansion. In 1955, during Gov. William Stratton's administration, other furnishings included a gold clock on the mantle, gold and crystal chandeliers, silver service with the state seal, candelabrum with the state seal, and chairs with the state seal. (Courtesy of Abraham Lincoln Presidential Library and Museum.)

From left to right, personnel director J. Elmore and business manager William Arnold of Bressmer's department store talk with George Winston, executive secretary of the Springfield Urban League, about hiring African Americans. Until 1958, Bressmer's hired no African Americans but eventually hired elevator operators, porters, and package wrappers. John Bressmer created the upscale downtown store in 1861. (Courtesy of Springfield Urban League Inc.)

Margaret Pendergrass attended Springfield High School and Hampton Institute School of Library Science. She worked at the Phyllis Wheatley Branch of the Greenville, South Carolina, library; Fort Custer, Michigan, camp library; and Illinois State Library as head of the juvenile department. In 1957, she attended an Illinois Library Association conference in Chicago where she presented the paper "Subject Heading in Special Libraries." (Courtesy of Springfield Urban League Inc.)

An unidentified man works at Bare Shoe Shop at 1207 East Washington Street. Emmett Bare owned the business from the 1940s to the 1960s. In 1943, a fire resulted in $50 worth of damage. In the 1960s, the shop moved to 146 South Wesley Street. It advertised the finest shoe work at unusually low prices. (Beverly Helm-Renfro.)

Alvin Rountree looks at an executive register in the third-floor stacks of the Illinois State Archives around 1957. Rountree was from East St. Louis and worked as an assistant archivist for 36 years. His community involvement included Goodwill Industries, Abraham Lincoln Association, Amvets, Frontiers International, Grace United Methodist Church, Alpha Phi Alpha fraternity, and the Urban League. (Courtesy of Illinois State Archives, Doc Helm Collection.)

This is the Helm family house at 1128 South Pasfield Street in the 1940s. It was in a white, middle-class neighborhood, although African Americans such as Mae Hammons, the first African American schoolteacher in Springfield, lived next door. The house had a basement photography studio used from 1947 to 1994. (Beverly Helm-Renfro.)

Four

ENTREPRENEURSHIP

In 1933, Sella La Fieleo (left) and John La Fieleo (right) were general managers of John Sella Air Motor Company at 126 East Jefferson Street. John invented a compressed air automobile motor, which he demonstrated for the public, promising a $125 weekly return on a $500 investment. The La Fieleos traveled throughout the country demonstrating the car, which operated without gasoline. (Courtesy of Abraham Lincoln Presidential Library and Museum.)

In the 1950s, Maurine Shipp (left) gives Dorothy Helm the annual African American women's bridge club award. Shipp worked for the Illinois Department of Agriculture for 24 years and established Shipp Real Estate Agency in 1965. She was a member of the Beta Gamma chapter of the Iota Phi Lambda sorority and selected as Springfield's outstanding businesswoman in 1988. (Beverly Helm-Renfro.)

Wabash Tavern was located at 1001 East Washington Street near the Wabash Railroad Company's Tenth Street tracks. It was operated by Albert Miles until the mid-1940s when he bought a different tavern. Employees behind the bar are, from left to right, Mildred Caldwell, Flabby Robinson, and Richard Robinson. (Beverly Helm-Renfro.)

Leon Stewart (left) was born in Springfield in 1901 and went into the service station business. His earliest station was at Fourteenth and Jefferson Streets in the 1920s and 1930s. In 1952, his station at 1400 East Jefferson Street was listed in *The Negro Motorist Green Book*. In 1980, Stewart was honored as the Copley First Citizen of Greater Springfield for his community service with groups such as the Boys Club and the Boy Scouts. (Beverly Helm-Renfro.)

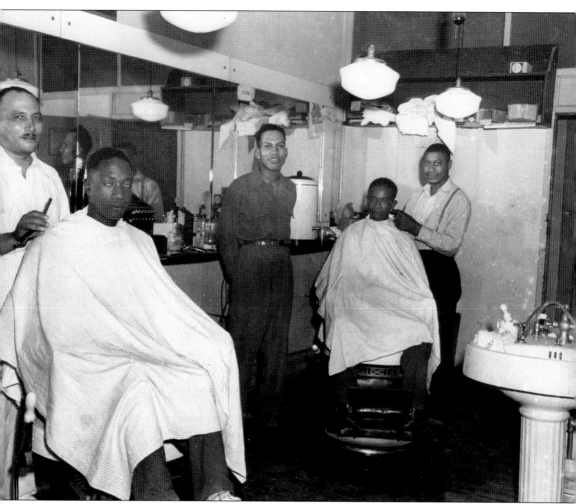

George Sykes (far right) was a barber for over 40 years and owned a barbershop at 120 South Eleventh Street, next to Hotel Dudley. Sykes sold tickets for Mahalia Jackson's performance at the Illinois State Armory in 1960. His shop became a popular gathering place for African American men and was listed in *The Negro Motorist Green Book* in 1952. (Beverly Helm-Renfro.)

Jim's Shining Parlor was at 209 South Sixth Street. From 1942 to 1944, the owner, Jimmie Haley (left), ran help-wanted advertisements in the *Daily Illinois State Register*. He was looking for experienced shoe shiners and promised steady work and good pay. The unidentified young man inside may have been an employee. (Beverly Helm-Renfro.)

Here, Dr. Webster works with an unidentified young patient and a woman. Webster was a dentist for over 40 years and had an office at 501 South Thirteenth Street in the 1960s. In 1969, at a testimonial dinner held at the St. Nicholas Hotel ballroom, Springfield saluted his years of service, particularly to youth. He examined orphans at the Lincoln Colored Home, founded in 1898 by Eva Carroll Monroe. (Courtesy of Springfield Urban League Inc.)

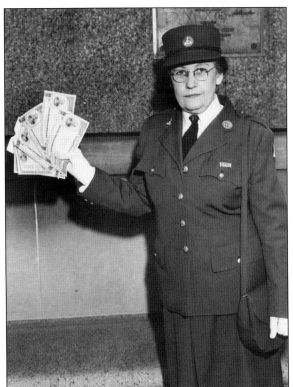

Mabel Pettiford lived at 120 South Eleventh Street where she also owned the Panama Tavern, which was listed in *The Negro Motorist Green Book* in the 1950s. Later, she owned the W.W. White-Pettiford Funeral Home at 1304 East Monroe Street. She was active in the Douglass Community Center, which offered civic, social, and educational opportunities for African Americans. Here, she sells war bonds during World War II. (Beverly Helm-Renfro.)

Dr. Edwin Lee received his medical degree in 1941 and eight years later moved to Springfield, where he worked as a surgeon and family practice physician. In 1972, he received Springfield's Copley First Citizen award. He founded Frontiers International, was president of the Springfield District 186 Board of Education, and was a lifetime member of the NAACP. (Courtesy of Springfield Urban League Inc.)

Rosalee Harris was proprietor of the Subway Club, a tavern and brothel at 1015 South Seventeenth Street. In 1950, Cab Calloway and his orchestra enjoyed a cocktail party and breakfast there. The club was listed in *The Negro Motorist Green Book* in 1952. Amid accusations of selling liquor to minors, the city closed her business down in 1955. (Beverly Helm-Renfro.)

Deluxe Café was at 1028 East Washington Street from the 1930s to 1950s and served hamburgers, hot dogs, chili, and Coca-Cola. It was a popular meeting place for African American civic organizations. They also sold tickets for African American performances. A soldier in uniform smokes a cigarette on the doorstep next door. (Beverly Helm-Renfro.)

Robert Krushall owned Krushall Cleaners at 1331 East Adams Street, next to his residence. This unidentified employee most likely worked there in the 1940s. Krushall was from Eagle Lake, Texas, and also worked at the Illinois secretary of state's office in Springfield. He was a member of St. John's African Methodist Episcopal Church. (Beverly Helm-Renfro.)

During the 1940s, Jesse Martin stands among flowers in Factor Greenhouse at 1608 South Grand Avenue East. He bought the greenhouse with his business partner, Lewis South, in 1944. It originally opened in the late 1800s and contained a house, barn, and heating boilers for the greenhouse. They sold carnations, delphiniums, daisies, pansies, vegetable plants, and strawberry plants. (Beverly Helm-Renfro.)

In 1938, Dr. Isaac English graduated from Meharry Medical College in Nashville, Tennessee, then worked for Homer G. Phillips Hospital in St. Louis. The hospital operated from the 1930s to the 1970s, serving African Americans during racial segregation. In 1941, Dr. English opened a general practice office at 212½ South Fifth Street in Springfield. His wife, Catherine, completed nursing school and is pictured with him. (Beverly Helm-Renfro.)

In 1973, Shirley Frye was chosen Sangamon County queen for Gamma Xi chapter of the Alpha Chi Pi Omega sorority and fraternity at their 28th annual national convention in Omaha, Nebraska. Later, she owned All Faces Beauty Salon at 1516 South Grand Avenue East. She lived at 54 Brandon Court, part of the Springfield Housing Authority. Jesse Hammer stands beside her in this photograph. (Beverly Helm-Renfro.)

Stephen Finnie returned to Springfield from the Army in 1919 after serving in Hawaii and Arizona as an operating room assistant with the 25th Infantry. By 1921, he ran undertaking services for African Americans at 300 South Eleventh Street. Two years later, he was a funeral director and licensed embalmer at Finnie-Wade Funeral Home, pictured here at 1425 East Adams Street. (Beverly Helm-Renfro.)

Members of the Cansler family pose on their farm near North Eighth Street and the Illinois State Fairgrounds. From the 1940s to 1960s, Leslie Cansler owned Cansler's Café and Cocktail Lounge at 807 (later 423) East Washington Street, part of a bustling strip of African American–owned clubs. It was listed in *The Negro Motorist Green Book* during the 1950s. (Beverly Helm-Renfro.)

Oscar Richie was born in Edwards, Mississippi, and married Gladys Brandon in 1952. The two are pictured here. Richie and his brother Boston owned Boston Richie Deluxe General Hauling Trucking Company in Springfield for nearly 80 years. Oscar was an Army veteran of World War II, member of Union Baptist Church, and member of the Otis B. Duncan American Legion Post No. 809. (Beverly Helm-Renfro.)

Hotel Brown was founded for African Americans in 1914 at 130 South Eleventh Street. In 1936, it became the Hotel Dudley, owned by Alexander Dudley. Many African American civic organizations met there and it was listed in *The Negro Travelers' Green Book* from the 1930s to the 1950s. Three unidentified women and two children relax on chairs in front. (Beverly Helm-Renfro.)

Five

MILITARY AND PUBLIC SAFETY

Harlan Watson was a Springfield police officer for 20 years, Democratic politician, and state worker. Controversial and colorful, he endured suspensions and dismissals during his career with the police department and was eventually promoted to detective in 1959. He lived and worked on the east side and was a member of St. John's African Methodist Episcopal Church, the Masons, and the Vagabonds Club. (Courtesy of Springfield Urban League Inc.)

In 1898, the 8th Illinois Infantry, Company H, poses with locals in San Luis, Cuba. During the Spanish-American War, the African American infantry buried Spanish corpses, returned 5,000 prisoners to Spain, constructed roads and bridges, repaired streets and plazas, improved sanitary conditions, revived business, and restored order. They were known for competent policing methods and generous treatment of women and children. (Courtesy of Abraham Lincoln Presidential Library and Museum.)

In 1898, during the Spanish-American War, the 8th Illinois Infantry, Companies E and F, stayed in these barracks at Palma Soriana in Cuba. The African American soldiers got along well with natives and learned Spanish. Eight of the soldiers married Cuban women, and some invested in local real estate. Cubans were welcome to participate in their meals, social activities, and religious services. (Courtesy of Abraham Lincoln Presidential Library and Museum.)

The 8th Illinois Infantry hospital in San Luis, Cuba, is pictured during the Spanish-American War in 1898. The infantry had the lowest casualty rate from disease among all African American units. Col. John Marshall did not tolerate regulation infractions and emphasized cleanliness and health. He tried to obtain fresh food and medicine for his troops, who in turn introduced Cubans to American standards of hygiene. (Courtesy of Abraham Lincoln Presidential Library and Museum.)

This is the 8th Illinois Infantry field hospital at Camp Marshall in San Luis, Cuba, during the 1898 Spanish-American War. Colonel Marshall is on his horse this Christmas morning. Because both the infantry officers and soldiers were African American, Marshall was under pressure to perform. He was a strict disciplinarian and held high standards for cleanliness, health, nutrition, behavior, and religion. (Courtesy of Abraham Lincoln Presidential Library and Museum.)

In 1901, this was the Illinois National Guard's 8th Illinois Infantry, Company A, at Camp Lincoln. It was the nation's first all–African American National Guard unit. The soldiers pictured here could have served in the Spanish-American War in Cuba. (Courtesy of Abraham Lincoln Presidential Library and Museum.)

In 1901, this was the Illinois National Guard's 8th Illinois Infantry, Company B, at Camp Lincoln. According to the 1901–1902 adjutant general's report, soldiers were issued breech-loading .45-caliber Springfield rifles along with bayonets. Three soldiers in the first row at left are also holding a drum and trumpets. (Courtesy of Abraham Lincoln Presidential Library and Museum.)

In 1901, this was the Illinois National Guard's 8th Illinois Infantry, Company C, at Camp Lincoln. According to the 1901–1902 adjutant general's report, their canteens and haversacks were in good order. Several men pictured here are wearing long and honorable service and marksmanship medals and badges. (Courtesy of Abraham Lincoln Presidential Library and Museum.)

In 1901, this was the Illinois National Guard's 8th Illinois Infantry, Company D, at Camp Lincoln. Their poses show informal camaraderie. A child (first row, right) and unidentified man (fourth row, right) are likely visiting from out of town to watch popular camp spectacles such as parades, athletics, swimming, music, and religious services. (Courtesy of Abraham Lincoln Presidential Library and Museum.)

Lt. Col. James H. Johnson (first row, center) poses with his medical staff in 1901 at Camp Lincoln. Doctors are beside him along with orderlies wearing red cross armbands. They were part of the Illinois National Guard's 8th Illinois Infantry—the nation's first all–African American National Guard unit. Johnson was from Chicago and served in the Spanish-American War in Cuba. (Courtesy of Abraham Lincoln Presidential Library and Museum.)

In 1902, three men work at the commissary at Camp Lincoln—the permanent encampment grounds for the Illinois National Guard. First built in 1886, soldiers from around Illinois trained on its sprawling 80 acres near Spring Creek. It originally included a rifle range, quartermaster's house, icehouse, stables, swimming pool, city water lines, and streetcar railways connecting it to the city. (Courtesy of Abraham Lincoln Presidential Library and Museum.)

In 1903, Lt. Col. James H. Johnson (first row, left) and Col. John R. Marshall (first row, center) pose with staff and color guard at Camp Lincoln as part of the Illinois National Guard's 8th Illinois Infantry. Marshall was a stonemason from Chicago who governed, rebuilt, and restored San Luis, Cuba, during the Spanish-American War. (Courtesy of Abraham Lincoln Presidential Library and Museum.)

Charles Grandy traveled alone from his home in Norfolk, Virginia, to attend the 1940 Grand Army of the Republic national encampment in Springfield. Grandy was enslaved but joined the Union forces during the Civil War. He was over six feet tall and weighed 250 pounds. At 98 years old, he may have marched or rode in the downtown parade during the encampment. (Courtesy of Abraham Lincoln Presidential Library and Museum.)

In the early 1940s, Legionnaires gather outside the Col. Otis B. Duncan American Legion Post No. 809 at 1127 East Monroe Street. Duncan was born in Springfield in 1873 and became the highest ranking African American officer in the American Expeditionary Forces in Europe during World War I. This new post would serve Legionnaires of World Wars I and II. (Beverly Helm-Renfro.)

In the 1940s, Marie Sublett stands outside the Centennial building. She was born in Springfield in 1899 and enlisted in the Women's Army Auxiliary Corps, where she received basic training. During her military career she was stationed at bases around the country and attended Washington and Lee University in Virginia, where she studied education. (Beverly Helm-Renfro.)

James Lewis enlisted during the Civil War in 1863 and served in Company B of the 3rd Negro Cavalry. In 1892, he received a law degree from Union College of Law, later Northwestern University College of Law, in Chicago. In 1942, he attended Illinois's 76th annual Grand Army of the Republic encampment in Springfield. At 102, he was the oldest attendee. (Courtesy of Abraham Lincoln Presidential Library and Museum.)

During the 1940s, Doc Helm photographed African Americans returning to Springfield from all branches of the military. From left to right are Jimmie, Bobby, and Harry Moore. Harry was a private in the Army and is buried in Camp Butler National Cemetery in Springfield. (Beverly Helm-Renfro.)

Floyd Stapleton was born in 1926 and served in the Navy during World War II. When he was in Springfield during the 1940s, Doc Helm took this picture in his commercial studio at 809 East Washington Street. Helm took many photographs of military personnel, male and female. Stapleton died at the age of 76 and is buried in Camp Butler National Cemetery in Springfield. (Beverly Helm-Renfro.)

Gov. William Stratton presents awards to two unidentified Veterans of Foreign Wars members from Post No. 5422 and Post No. 730 on Veterans Day at the state fair on August 16, 1959. In the background are drill teams, bands, and bugle corps. (Courtesy of Illinois State Archives, Doc Helm Collection.)

This is Firehouse No. 5 at 1310 East Adams Street in the early 1940s. From left to right are (first row) Charles Lockhart, two unidentified, and Noble Alexander; (second row) Robert Shields, Harry McNeil, LaRue Willis, and ? Young. This firehouse served the southeast section of the city, which grew rapidly with industry in the 1930s. (Beverly Helm-Renfro.)

Robert Shields worked at Andy's Shining Parlor until he became a firefighter with Firehouse No. 5 at 1310 East Adams Street in 1940. He recalled it was a good job, as his colleagues became the best firefighters in the city. In 1954, Firehouse No. 5 moved to Eighteenth and Clay Streets, and integration of the Springfield Fire Department began two years later. (Beverly Helm-Renfro.)

During the first week of June 1942, Central Metal & Iron Company reported 10 tons of rubber stolen from its junkyard at 216 North Seventh Street. Later that month, the United States held a two-week rubber drive, paying 1¢ per pound. During the drive, Sangamon County sheriff Harry Eielson (center) stands with five unidentified men suspected of tire theft. (Courtesy of Abraham Lincoln Presidential Library and Museum.)

Charles Lockhart (left) meets with Frederick O'Hara, city commissioner in the late 1950s. Lockhart was born in 1903 in Mammoth, West Virginia, and came to Springfield in 1921. He began working for the fire department in 1929 and retired in 1966 as deputy fire chief. He also coached Golden Gloves boxers from 1930 until the mid-1940s and was associated with the Firehouse No. 5 team. (Beverly Helm-Renfro.)

In the 1950s, this group of officers would have attended the Illinois State Police Academy in Springfield. Gathered in Chicago, they are demonstrating a new and innovative radar system. By 1962, Prince Preston (far left) was assigned to District 13 at Du Quoin with residence in Sparta. Five years later, he was promoted from trooper to corporal with a pay increase from $590 to $620 monthly. (Courtesy of Robert Moore.)

The first annual Illinois State Police invitational pistol match was held in 1960 at the state fair in Springfield. Robert Patton, second from left, won sixth place out of 150 marksmen from the Midwest. The National Rifle Association supervised the three-day competition where officers used .22-, .38-, and .45-caliber weapons. Patton, who was from Chicago, had been promoted to lieutenant in 1958. (Courtesy of Illinois State Archives, Doc Helm Collection.)

Robert Moore (right) was born in 1943 in Algoma, Mississippi. He moved to Illinois in 1965 and in 1976 was affirmative action officer for the Illinois State Police, traveling throughout the state recruiting minority youth. Here, he talks with children in Alton. Moore later became president of the Illinois Affirmative Action Officers Association, a US marshal under Pres. Bill Clinton, and chief of police in Jackson, Mississippi. (Courtesy of Robert Moore.)

Six

POLITICS

Portia Washington Pittman (left), daughter of Booker T. Washington, presents Gov. Dwight Green a Booker T. Washington memorial half dollar in 1947 at the governor's office. Eugene Shands stands behind them. The coin was issued in 1946 and reissued annually until 1951. African American artist Isaac Scott Hathaway designed Washington's portrait on the front and his log cabin birthplace on the back. (Courtesy of Illinois State Archives, Doc Helm Collection.)

In November 1890, Dr. George Wellington Bryant visited Lincoln's tomb and spoke to hundreds of Republicans gathered at Turner Hall on East Jefferson Street. Bryant was enslaved in Kentucky, joined the Union army, and later became an orator. By 1891, he headed the National Emancipation Monument Association for the 1893 world's fair in Chicago. Sculptor Lorado Taft designed the proposed monument. (Courtesy of Brookens Library.)

Richard Yates Sr. supported Abraham Lincoln and became Illinois's Civil War governor. His son Richard Yates Jr. was governor from 1901 to 1904. In 1902, he deployed state militia to suppress a race riot in Eldorado and passed a child labor law limiting work hours. At this 1904 rally outside the governor's mansion stands an African American child (fourth row, far right). (Courtesy of Abraham Lincoln Presidential Library and Museum.)

In 1935, the Young Republicans of Illinois led a pilgrimage to New Salem State Park to honor Abraham Lincoln, the father of their party. Jerome Singleton (left, in black suit) conducts the Lincoln Liberty Chorus in singing "Deep River" and "When You Come Out the Wilderness." A special Chicago & Midland train transported attendees from the Illinois Central Depot at Sixth and Madison Streets in Springfield. (Courtesy of Abraham Lincoln Presidential Library and Museum.)

In the governor's office at the Illinois State Capitol are, from left to right, Rep. Corneal Davis, Gov. Dwight Green, and Rep. Fred Smith signing House Bill No. 251 on June 29, 1945. It read, "History of the Negro race may be taught in all public schools and in all other educational institutions in this State supported or maintained, in whole or in part, by public funds." (Courtesy of Illinois State Archives, Doc Helm Collection.)

On February 9, 1947, three days before Abraham Lincoln's birthday, from left to right, Rev. George Winston, unidentified, Rev. Henry Blakey, and Dr. Martin Bickham made a pilgrimage to Lincoln's tomb. Winston was cochairman of the Race Relations Committee of Springfield Council of Churches, and Bickham was chairman of the Illinois Interracial Commission. At the tomb, Blakey offered a prayer for racial reconciliation. (Courtesy of Springfield Urban League Inc.)

A statewide action conference for the enactment of an Illinois Fair Employment Practice law was held on March 18, 1947, at the St. Nicholas Hotel at 400 East Jefferson Street. Pres. Franklin D. Roosevelt enacted the federal legislation, which helped African Americans and other minorities obtain higher skilled and higher paying jobs in the World War II economy. (Courtesy of Springfield Urban League Inc.)

Sterling Tucker (left) meets with Gov. Adlai Stevenson at the governor's mansion in 1952. Tucker was born in Akron, Ohio, and attended the University of Akron for his degrees in sociology and psychology. He worked for the National Urban League and organized Solidarity Day for the Poor People's Campaign in 1969. Pres. Jimmy Carter appointed him assistant secretary of the Department of Housing and Urban Development in 1979. (Courtesy of Springfield Urban League Inc.)

In 1953, Joseph Bibb became the first African American to hold a cabinet post in Illinois. Gov. William Stratton appointed him director of the department of public safety, which included prisons, state police, pardon boards, and parole boards. Bibb was an attorney and managing editor of a newspaper in Chicago. Here, he addresses a Springfield Urban League forum. (Courtesy of Springfield Urban League Inc.)

Gov. William Stratton and his wife, Shirley Stratton (first row, third from left), hosted a luncheon at the governor's mansion on June 3, 1959. Seventy women members of the Republican Central Committee of Cook County traveled to Springfield on an Illinois Central train to visit Abraham Lincoln sites and watch the legislature in session. It was the first large group of its kind to make this trip. (Courtesy of Abraham Lincoln Presidential Library and Museum.)

In 1959, female legislators meet at the governor's mansion with Shirley Stratton, the governor's wife. From left to right are Lillian Schlagenhauf, Floy Clements, Marguerite Church, Jeanne Hurley, Ferne Pierce, Frances Dawson, Esther Saperstein, Stratton, Lottie O'Neill, and Lillian Piotrowski. In 1958, Clements, a Democrat from Chicago, was the first African American woman elected to the Illinois General Assembly. (Courtesy of Abraham Lincoln Presidential Library and Museum.)

On the first legislative day of 1959, Sen. Fred Smith, a Democrat from Chicago, stands at the senate rostrum in the Illinois State Capitol building with two family members. In 1961, Smith sponsored fair employment practices legislation, creating a five-member commission to investigate allegations of prejudicial hiring by firms with more than 25 employees. It was part of Gov. William Stratton's legislative program. (Courtesy of Illinois State Archives, Doc Helm Collection.)

Rep. Cecil Partee, a Democrat from Chicago, sits in the Illinois State Capitol house lounge with family members. Partee attended Tennessee State University and Northwestern University School of Law and served as assistant state's attorney in Cook County. In 1961, Partee sponsored an open occupancy bill to end discrimination in housing. (Courtesy of Illinois State Archives, Doc Helm Collection.)

In 1961, Charles Carpentier (left) and Doc Helm shake hands on the Illinois State Capitol steps in front of the Abraham Lincoln statue. Carpentier was the Republican secretary of state from 1953 to 1964. Helm, wearing a camera and flash, worked for the secretary of state under various Republican and Democratic directors. Early in his career he also raised and lowered the flag at the Illinois State Capitol. (Courtesy of Illinois State Archives, Doc Helm Collection.)

Gov. Otto Kerner (seated) signs the Fair Employment Practices Act on July 21, 1961, in the governor's office at the Illinois State Capitol. From left to right are Rep. Charles Armstrong, Rep. Cecil Partee, Rep. Corneal Davis, Rep. James Carter, Rep. Horace Gardner, Sen. Fred Smith, Rep. William Robinson, unidentified, Rep. Elwood Graham, and two unidentified. (Courtesy of Illinois State Archives, Doc Helm Collection.)

Eleven agricultural extension specialists from Sierra Leone, Nigeria, Sudan, Liberia, and the West Indies toured the 1962 Illinois State Fair. A new international trade section highlighted Illinois grains exported to 21 foreign countries. For this picture, the visitors gathered in Democratic governor Otto Kerner's reception office at the Illinois State Capitol. (Courtesy of Illinois State Archives, Doc Helm Collection.)

Abraham Lincoln's Emancipation Proclamation took effect in 1863. One hundred years later in 1963, the Illinois State Fair created a Land of Lincoln exhibit in the pavilion. Internationally renowned gospel singer Mahalia Jackson (right) and United Nations ambassador Adlai Stevenson III (center poster) were invited speakers. They gathered at the Democratic State Central Committee of Illinois headquarters at 123 North Fourth Street. (Beverly Helm-Renfro.)

In 1974, the Black Caucus gathered in the Illinois State Capitol. From left to right are (first row) Fred Smith, Wyvetter Young, Cecil Partee, Corneal Davis, Kenneth Hall, and Richard Newhouse; (second row) Eugene Barnes, Emil Jones, Charles Gaines, Bill Robinson, James McLendon, unidentified, and Raymond Ewell; (third row) Jesse White, Harold Washington, unidentified, Taylor Pouncey, and James Taylor. (Beverly Helm-Renfro.)

From left to right are Illinois senator Charles Chew, US senator Joseph Biden, and Illinois senator Phil Rock. Biden was attending a Democratic fundraiser at Holiday Inn East on June 12, 1974. Chew was a Chicago city alderman who later focused on civil rights and transportation issues as a senator. (Courtesy of Illinois State Archives, Doc Helm Collection.)

In 1975, Beverly Helm (left) was working for state senator Fred Smith, a Democrat from Chicago. His colleague, state senator Charles Chew, brought Muhammad Ali to Springfield. Beverly's father, Doc Helm, took several pictures of his daughter and Ali together. Beverly's colleague Barb Esela (right) worked for another state senator in the Centennial building. (Beverly Helm-Renfro.)

Seven

URBAN LEAGUE

In 1940, the Springfield Urban League had a nursery for working mothers where their children received one hot meal a day. There were also fruit and vegetable gardens as well as a barn converted into a program area for dancing and other activities. (Courtesy of Springfield Urban League Inc.)

Comer Cox (first row, sixth from left) was born in Athens, Alabama, and later moved to St. Louis, Missouri, where he played high school baseball and football in the 1920s when this photograph was taken. He later graduated with a business degree from Fisk University in Nashville, Tennessee, and played Negro League baseball in 1930 and 1931. At the end of a long career serving African American organizations, he became executive director of the Springfield Urban League from 1962 until his death in 1971. (Courtesy of Abraham Lincoln Presidential Library and Museum.)

This portrait of Minnie Pettiford was taken on September 16, 1932, during the Douglass Community Center golf club's annual tournament at Bunn Park. In 1931, Pettiford won the women's trophy. The club held soirees at the Imperial Temple at 120 South Eleventh Street. (Courtesy of Abraham Lincoln Presidential Library and Museum.)

In 1935, the mother's club of the Springfield Urban League nursery school held a jitney supper at the main headquarters at 234 South Fifteenth Street. Jitney suppers were fundraisers where food was sold by the scoop for one nickel. The club also held benefit valentine teas. Lethia Stapleton was president. (Courtesy of Springfield Urban League Inc.)

The citizens committee of the Springfield Urban League held its sixth annual old folks picnic at Lake Springfield's Bridgeview Beach on June 29, 1939. George Donnegan, who shook Abraham Lincoln's hand in 1861 when he left Springfield for the last time to be inaugurated as president, was

there. Attendees took a drive around the lake and listened to the Springfield Colored Municipal Band. (Courtesy of Springfield Urban League Inc.)

In 1940, African American and white youth cut, stenciled, and painted city and state park signs at the Springfield Urban League building. The purpose was to teach racial tolerance so African American children would feel they had a place in American society. The National Youth Administration also taught them how to paint luminous signs for highways. (Courtesy of Springfield Urban League Inc.)

The Illinois Urban League held its fifth annual youth conference in Springfield on June 29, 1940. City, state, and national government agencies; the Hull House in Chicago; and the National Negro Alliance sent speakers to discuss civil liberties, employment, voting, war, and peace. The 150 participants danced at the Royal Gardens in the evening and attended a mass meeting in the Centennial building the next day. (Courtesy of Springfield Urban League Inc.)

From 1931 to 1942, Oliver Jerome Singleton directed the Douglass Community Center. In 1935, he sponsored a weeklong musical institute headed by the National Recreation Association in hopes of creating a permanent music institute for African Americans. Later, he became recreation director for the Springfield Urban League and worked at the Illiopolis defense plant during World War II. He is pictured here with Virginia Harris, who shared his office. (Courtesy of Springfield Urban League Inc.)

In the mid-1940s, the Springfield Urban League building at 234 South Fifteenth Street was known as the Old Gray Lady. It provided meeting space for groups such as the NAACP and the Young Women's Christian Association Phyllis Wheatley Club. Programming revolved around arts and crafts, community speakers, dance, drama, education, health, music, and sports. (Beverly Helm-Renfro.)

Rev. George Winston was educated at historically black Lincoln University in Pennsylvania and became executive secretary of the Springfield Urban League in 1945. As an ordained Baptist minister, he was also part-time pastor at Zion Baptist Church. His sermons and speeches included "In the Hands of the Master," "Good Will, How the Home Can Help in Guidance," and "Making Democracy Live." (Courtesy of Springfield Urban League Inc.)

Edythe Grady and two unidentified men stand at the Douglass Community Center at 234 South Fifteenth Street. Grady attended Webster University in Kansas City, Missouri. As director of the center from approximately 1945 to 1955, she supervised entertainment for children and adults. The Springfield Urban League remained there from 1934 to 1961. (Beverly Helm-Renfro.)

The Springfield Urban League held its annual meeting on December 10, 1946, at Union Baptist Church at 1401 East Monroe Street. Thomas Paris, president of the board, gave the principal address. The Springfield Colored Municipal Band played, and a men's choral group from Union Baptist Church sang. (Courtesy of Springfield Urban League Inc.)

Dr. Lester Granger, executive secretary of the National Urban League, speaks at the annual meeting of the Springfield Urban League held at the Young Men's Christian Association at 317 South Seventh Street in 1948. Granger's topic was "More Unfinished Business for American Leadership." He organized the Los Angeles chapter of the National Urban League. Langdon Robinson, Granger's former classmate from Dartmouth College, is seated at left. (Courtesy of Springfield Urban League Inc.)

Lucius Harper (right) was executive editor of the *Chicago Defender* newspaper. He was known for his regular column *Dustin' Off the News* about world travel, history, and current events. At the Springfield Urban League's annual meeting in 1949, he was guest speaker on the topic "The Real Reconstruction." The meeting was held at the Centennial building auditorium at the corner of Edwards and Second Streets. An unidentified man stands beside him. (Courtesy of Springfield Urban League Inc.)

The Springfield Urban League and Springfield Commission on Human Relations cosponsored a human relations workshop at the Leland Hotel in 1951. The theme was "Strengthening Democracy on the Home Front." The keynote speaker was Rev. Archibald Carey—Chicago alderman, lawyer, minister, and civic leader. Clinics were held on public accommodations, education and recreation, and employment. (Courtesy of Springfield Urban League Inc.)

The Springfield Urban League held its 30th annual meeting on December 11, 1956, at the Hotel Abraham Lincoln at Fifth Street and Capitol Avenue. Leo Bohanon, director of the St. Louis Urban League, spoke about the positive aspects of integration. The Acolian Ensemble, directed by Dorothy Sims Winston, sang "By the Streams of Babylon" and "The Echo Song." (Courtesy of Springfield Urban League Inc.)

The Springfield Urban League recognized Equal Opportunity Day to commemorate Lincoln's Gettysburg Address given November 19, 1863. Seated from left to right are Louis Quonn, Mayor Lester Collins, Dr. Webster, and George Hoffman, with unidentified men standing behind them. In 1959, the league recognized Myers Brothers, Bressmer's, Kroger, and Illinois Bell for hiring African Americans. (Courtesy of Springfield Urban League Inc.)

In 1968, the Springfield Urban League, Springfield School District, and Association of Commerce and Industry cosponsored Occupational Happenings Career Day at Lanphier High School. All city school students could attend and learn about 27 career categories, view exhibits, and listen to speakers. (Courtesy of Sangamon Valley Collection at Lincoln Library.)

In the late 1960s, the Springfield Urban League guild scholarship awarded $500 to unmarried high school graduates of moral worth with at least a 3.0 grade point average to attend any accredited university. From left to right are Leola Smallwood, Geraldine Lee, Charlotte Woodson, Lois Shelton, Dorothy Winston, Bernice Pryor, Carrie Shaw, Georgia Perkins, Gladys Redd, Elma Webster, Charlotte Berry, and Opal Dixon at an annual tea. (Courtesy of Springfield Urban League Inc.)

Springfield Urban League held its 46th annual meeting on December 7, 1972, at Holiday Inn East. The theme was "The Search for Equality." From left to right are Mayor William Telford, two unidentified, board president Alvin Rountree, and executive director Howard Veal. Vernon Jordan, president of the National Urban League, was guest speaker. During that time, the Springfield Urban League offered scholarships, tutoring, job interviewing, counseling, and referrals. (Courtesy of Sangamon Valley Collection at Lincoln Library.)

DISCOVER THOUSANDS OF LOCAL HISTORY BOOKS FEATURING MILLIONS OF VINTAGE IMAGES

Arcadia Publishing, the leading local history publisher in the United States, is committed to making history accessible and meaningful through publishing books that celebrate and preserve the heritage of America's people and places.

Find more books like this at
www.arcadiapublishing.com

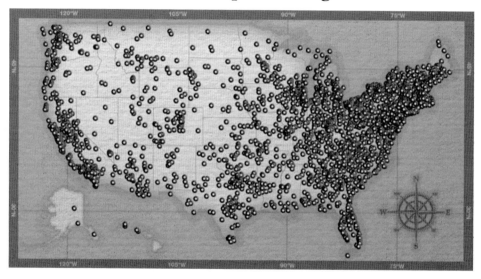

Search for your hometown history, your old stomping grounds, and even your favorite sports team.